Contents

Words appearing in the text in bold, **like this**, are explained in the Glossary.

 Find out more about Pakistan at www.heinemannexplore.co.uk

Where is Pakistan?

To learn more about Pakistan we meet three children who live there. Pakistan is a country in Asia. It is near India and China.

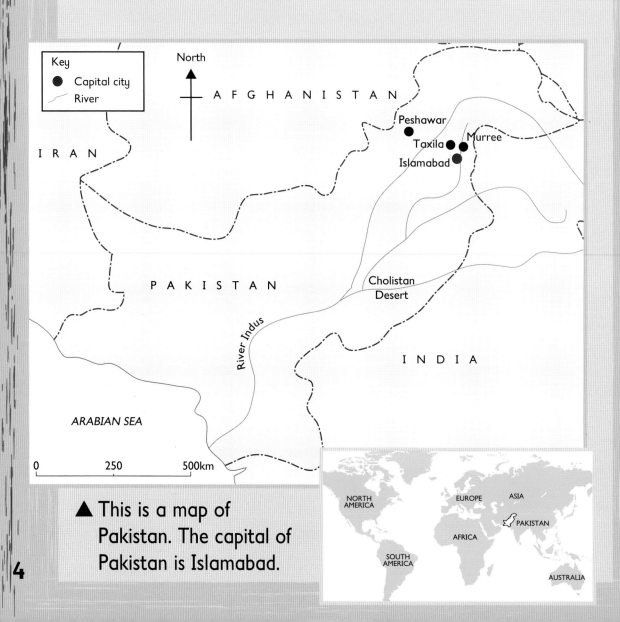

Key
● Capital city
〜 River

North

AFGHANISTAN

IRAN

Peshawar

Taxila ● ● Murree

Islamabad

PAKISTAN

Cholistan Desert

River Indus

INDIA

ARABIAN SEA

0   250   500km

NORTH AMERICA   EUROPE   ASIA

PAKISTAN

AFRICA

SOUTH AMERICA

AUSTRALIA

▲ This is a map of Pakistan. The capital of Pakistan is Islamabad.

The weather in Pakistan is mostly hot, but it can be cold in the north. Sometimes there are **earthquakes** in Pakistan. At certain times of the year there are also **monsoons**.

▼ There are busy towns in Pakistan.

▼ Most people in Pakistan live in the countryside.

Meet Kynat

Kynat is eight years old. She lives in Islamabad, the capital city of Pakistan. Kynat lives with her mother, father and older sister.

Kynat's father

Kynat's mother

Kynat

Kynat's sister

Kynat's mother makes ▶
chapattis for the family.

In the evening, the family eat a meal together. Kynat's mother cooks the food. The family likes to eat rice, **chapattis** and curry.

Kynat's school

Kynat goes to school six days a week. She learns maths, English, **Urdu** and art. Kynat likes English but she does not like maths.

▲ There are 50 children in Kynat's class.

Kynat's class practise cricket and hockey in the school yard. At playtime, Kynat plays clapping and skipping games with her friends.

◀ Kynat and her sister play skipping games at home too.

9

Having fun

When Kynat is not at school, she likes flying her kite. The roof of Kynat's house is flat. Kynat and her sister can play on the roof. Kynat flies her kite there.

◀ For festivals Kynat has **henna** painted on her hands.

Kynat wears a long shirt and loose trousers. This is called a *shalwar kameez*. For **festivals**, like **Eid**, she wears a special *shalwar kameez*.

Festivals

There are many **festivals** in Pakistan. People and animals wear special clothes at festival time. They eat food sold at stalls on the street. Sometimes they dance too.

kite

Every year there is a kite festival in Pakistan. On kite day, lots of people fly their kites. There are hundreds of kites in the sky!

Meet Omar

Omar is seven years old. He lives in a city called Peshawar. Omar lives with his mother, father, younger brother, grandparents, three uncles and two aunts.

▼ Omar has a large family.

Omar's father

Omar's grandparents

Omar's mother

Omar's brother

Omar

Omar's father makes new clothes for people. He is a **tailor**. His mother works at home. Omar would like to be a doctor when he grows up.

Omar's father is very busy ▶ making new clothes before the **festival** of **Eid**.

At home

Omar likes to help his mother. He looks after his younger brother, Mosseen, while his mother does her work. He likes playing games with Mosseen.

Omar's favourite food is black-eyed beans and naan bread. His family buy food at the fair when it comes to town. Omar likes to drink the fresh fruit juice that is made at the fair.

Omar's day

Omar goes to school in the mornings. He has to wear a school uniform. In the afternoon, Omar goes to a class to study the **Qur'an** for an hour.

Omar and his best friend, ▶ Muzammin, are learning to read the Qur'an.

Omar likes looking after his pet birds.
He is also learning to play cricket.
Sometimes he watches cartoons with
his brother.

◄ Omar keeps his
pet birds on the
roof of his house.

19

Travelling in Pakistan

In the towns people travel in cars. They also travel in large buses. It is cheap to travel in **rickshaws** and in horse-drawn cars.

The buses in Pakistan ▶ can be very colourful.

In the country, there are not many buses or cars so people have to walk. People often walk a long way. Sometimes they carry things on their head as they walk. They also ride on camels.

This girl finds it easier to ▶ hold the heavy pot on her head than in her arms.

Meet Shazia

Shazia is eight years old. She lives in a small village called Cholistan. Shazia lives with her mother, father, brothers, sister, uncle and aunt.

Shazia's mother

Shazia's aunt

Shazia's sister

Shazia

Shazia's uncle

Shazia's father

Shazia's brothers

Cholistan is in ▶ the **desert**.

Shazia's parents are farmers. ▶
They own a small shop too.

Shazia's house is made of mud, wood and straw. They have no water or electricity in the house. There is lots of land around the house where Shazia can play.

Life in Cholistan

Shazia and her family look forward to two special **festivals**. One is **Eid** and the other is a spring festival. When there is a festival, Shazia wears a new *shalwar kameez*.

▼ Shazia is learning to sew, so she can make her own *shalwar kameez*.

Cholistan is the hottest, driest part of Pakistan. In the summer there is very little water. Shazia's family have to get water from a deep well. They also have a camel.

▲ Shazia's family have a camel. Camels can store water so they do not get thirsty very often.

School and work

Shazia's school only has one class. Shazia and her brothers and sister are all taught together. They have their lessons outside. Lessons are taught in **Urdu**.

Shazia walks to school with her father and brother. ▶

After school, Shazia sometimes helps in her parents' shop. She also feeds the farm animals, and helps her mother with the cooking.

▲ The goats are Shazia's favourite animals.

Places to visit

2000 years ago, many people travelled across Pakistan buying and selling silk. The road they travelled on became famous. It was called the Silk Road. Taxila was a city on the Silk Road.

▼ Today, people visit the old buildings at Taxila.

◀ Silk and sewing are still important in Pakistan.

cable car

There is a good view of Murree from the cable car. ▶

Murree is a city in the hills. People visit it in the summer because it is cooler than other parts of Pakistan. They travel up the hill by **cable car**.

Pakistani fact file

Flag

Capital city

Islamabad

Money

Rupee

Religion
• Around 97 percent of people in Pakistan are Muslims.

Language
• **Urdu** is the official language of Pakistan, but people also speak Punjabi, Sindhi, Siraiki, Pashtu and English.

Try speaking Urdu!
Subah bakhair .... Good morning.
Kaysay ho? .... How are you?
Bohatt shukria .... Thanks a lot.

 Find out more about Pakistan at
www.heinemannexplore.co.uk

Glossary

cable car car that moves along an overhead cable to take people up and down mountains

chapatti thin, flat bread

desert very hot, dry area of land that has almost no rain and very few plants

earthquake sudden movement of the ground caused by rocks under the earth

Eid Eid means celebration and is a very important time for Muslims. Eid-Al-Fitr is at the end of Ramadan, the month of fasting.

festival big celebration for a town or country

henna reddish dye that comes from the leaves of the henna plant

monsoon season of heavy rain

Qur'an Muslim holy book

rickshaw two wheeled cart with a hood, pulled by one or two people

tailor someone who makes clothes

Urdu official language of Pakistan

More books to read

Fiesta: Pakistan, I Dore, (Franklin Watts, 2001)

Country Insights: Pakistan, Eaniqa Khan and Rob Unwin, (Hodder Wayland, 2000)

Index